2021

MW00904833

BLUE Banner BIOGRAPHIES

BRADLEY COOPER

Kerrily Sapet

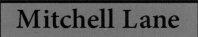

Mitchell Lane
PUBLISHERS
mitchelllane.com

2001 SW 31st Avenue
Hallandale, FL 33009

First Edition, 2021.
Author: Kerrily Sapet
Designer: Ed Morgan
Editor: Morgan Brody

Series: Blue Banner Biographies
Title: Bradley Cooper / by Kerrily Sapet

Hallandale, FL : Mitchell Lane Publishers, [2021]

Library bound ISBN: 978-1-68020-619-7
eBook ISBN: 978-1-68020-620-3

Contents

The Movie

BRADLEY COOPER sat on the couch next to his father. Images from a black and white movie flickered in the darkness. Cooper gazed at the actors on the screen and listened to the music. The movie, called *The Elephant Man*, told the true story of a man who suffered from severe physical deformities. Tears rolled down Cooper's face as he watched the movie.

Bradley Cooper is one of Hollywood's most recognizable actors.

Cooper was twelve years old. He understood what it was like to feel different from other people. Cooper had undergone several surgeries on one of his ears to repair a problem that could cause deafness. He worried whether people liked him. "I always found that I was never good enough in my own mind as to what I thought I should be," Cooper said. As Cooper watched *The Elephant Man*, he realized that movies could tell important stories and help people to understand each other. At that moment, Cooper decided he wanted to be an actor.

Anthony Hopkins (*left*) and John Hurt (*right*) starred in the 1980 movie *The Elephant Man.*

Cooper spent hours watching movies at the theater across the street from his house. He saw some movies as many as 30 times. Cooper studied the acting and tried to recreate the scenes in his backyard. He continued to think about *The Elephant Man.* "The movie just floored me—the music, the filmmaking, his story, everything," Cooper said.

When Cooper was in college, he discovered the movie *The Elephant Man* was based on a play about a man named Joseph Merrick. Cooper read the play again and again. He saved money and flew to London, England to learn more about Merrick, who died in 1890. Cooper visited the hospital where Merrick lived and the gardens where he walked at night so nobody could see him.

When Cooper returned, he staged a small performance of the play *The Elephant Man*. Cooper's father was in the audience. He had worried his son was making a mistake choosing acting as a career. Watching Cooper's performance changed his mind. "You're doing the right thing," Cooper's father said.

Starring in *The Elephant Man* was just the start of Bradley Cooper's career. One day he would perform the play on Broadway in front of huge crowds. Today, Cooper is one of the world's most famous stars, playing leading roles in TV shows and movies. Even though Cooper has written and directed award-winning movies, he has never forgotten *The Elephant Man*. That black and white movie made him want to be a part of the storytelling magic of the big screen.

From Ninja to Actor

BRADLEY **CHARLES** **COOPER** was born on January 5, 1975 in Jenkintown, Pennsylvania. His father, Charles, was a stockbroker. His mother, Gloria, worked at a local NBC TV station. Bradley also had an older sister named Holly.

Growing up, Bradley loved watching movies with his father. The two ate popcorn together as they watched and talked about the movies. They made up a game they called, "Would You Put Him in the Movie or Her in the Movie?" and each tried to name the best actor for a part. They also imagined an "ultimate film" with all of their favorite actors.

Cooper loves cooking and got the chance to play a chef in the 2015 movie *Burnt.*

Bradley also liked music and cooking. He listened to everything from classical to rock music. He played the bass, sometimes practicing on the way to school with the neck of the tall stringed instrument sticking out of the car window. On the weekends, Bradley and his grandmother often cooked together, making homemade pasta and ravioli. They liked, "taking whatever was in the fridge and turning it into lasagna," Bradley said.

CHAPTER **TWO**

One of Bradley's grandfathers was a fireman. The other was a policeman. Bradley loved their uniforms and was fascinated with soldiers because of the war movies he watched with his father. Bradley often lay on his stomach in his room, playing with toy soldiers and rumpling up the carpet to make different landscapes for their battles. He wanted to attend a nearby military school or move to Japan to train to be a ninja, but his parents said no.

Bradley thought about becoming a soldier, a ninja, a chef, or a musician. When he decided to become an actor, everything changed. "Movies moved me in a way that nothing else had at that point in my life," Bradley said. His activities—from playing an instrument to planning scenes with toy soldiers—gave him experiences he would use one day as an actor and director.

Bradley attended Germantown Academy. He was a good student and especially liked studying English. He played basketball and was on the tennis team. Bradley didn't try out for high school plays because he was afraid to try acting. Instead, he worked at the *Philadelphia Daily News* newspaper as an intern. In 1993, when Bradley graduated from high school, he decided to attend Villanova University. Bradley wasn't sure what his future held, but he hoped it would involve acting.

Cooper arrives at the 2012 Toronto International Film Festival.

Leaving Home

VILLANOVA UNIVERSITY in Philadelphia, Pennsylvania was close to Bradley Cooper's home. He soon realized though that the school wasn't a good fit. Villanova didn't have a theater program and he was ready to try acting. Cooper transferred to Georgetown University in Washington D.C. He attended classes, studied, and performed plays with Nomadic Theatre, a student theater group. He also joined the rowing team and spent six months in France as a foreign exchange student.

The New School is located at a busy street corner in New York City.

When Cooper graduated in 1997, he decided to take a chance and pursue acting. Cooper applied to the Actors Studio Drama School at The New School in New York City. The school had one of the best acting, directing, and playwriting programs in the country. Cooper was surprised and excited when he was accepted.

Actor Robert DeNiro is one of Cooper's idols.

At The New School, Cooper studied acting, voice, and movement. He learned from famous actors, such as Robert DeNiro. At night, Cooper worked at the nearby Morgan Hotel, where well-known actors, such as Leonardo DiCaprio, often stayed. One of Cooper's jobs was to light candles in the lobby before guests arrived. On the weekends, he volunteered with a program that taught acting to kids.

Cooper impressed his acting coach, Elizabeth Kemp, and the head of the school, James Lipton. "He's going to go all the way," Lipton told Cooper's father. "I never predicted that for any other student."

While Cooper was a student at The New School, he auditioned for roles on television shows. His first part was on the popular TV series *Sex and the City*. Bradley was so nervous he brushed his teeth 18 times before a scene in which he kissed the show's main character. Next, he got a part on the Discovery Channel show *Extreme Treks in a Wild World*. His adventures included kayaking with orcas (killer whales) in British Columbia and ice climbing in the Andes. Cooper hoped the small roles would help him score bigger parts in TV shows and movies.

In 2000, Cooper graduated from The New School and moved to Los Angeles, California. He was following the dream he'd had since he was young. But Cooper was one of many young actors hoping to get his big break in Hollywood.

CHAPTER **FOUR**

The Big Break

IN 2001, Bradley Cooper landed his first movie role. He played a camp counselor in the movie *Wet Hot American Summer*. Soon after, he got a part on *Alias*, a popular spy action TV show. He played a reporter named Will Tippin. People began to notice Cooper as an actor. His time on the show didn't last long though. When the show's writers started writing fewer scenes for his character, Cooper left the show.

In Cooper's movie debut, he appeared as the character Ben, a counselor at Camp Firewood.

Cooper had trouble finding other work. Making matters worse, a few weeks later, he tore his Achilles tendon while playing basketball. Cooper spent his days lying on the couch. He began to struggle with addiction to alcohol. Cooper was miserable and even wondered if he should quit acting. Cooper decided he wasn't ready to give up yet. He stopped drinking alcohol and continued to audition for parts.

CHAPTER **FOUR**

Over the next few years, Cooper played small roles in movies and on TV shows. In 2005, his dedication paid off when he landed a big role in the movie *The Wedding Crashers*. The movie was a huge success, earning almost $300 million worldwide. More work followed. Cooper appeared on television shows, such as *Kitchen Confidential* and *Nip/Tuck*. He also scored parts in movies, such as *Failure to Launch* and *The Rocker*.

Although Cooper's career was taking off, his personal life was rocky. In 2006, he married Jennifer Esposito, an actress, but they divorced four months later. Not long after, Cooper's father was diagnosed with lung cancer. Cooper eventually moved back to Philadelphia to care for his father, who died in 2011.

In 2009, Cooper landed his biggest role yet in the movie *The Hangover*. He played one of three friends on a trip to Las Vegas. The movie was wildly popular. It made $467 million. Cooper received an award at the 13th Hollywood Film Festival. He would star in the movie's two sequels.

Cooper promotes *The Hangover Part II*, in 2011.

Some of Cooper's movies were flops, such as *All About Steve*. He won the Golden Raspberry Award for the *Worst Screen Combo* with Sandra Bullock. Most of his movies, such as *The A-Team*, *Silver Linings Playbook*, and *American Hustle*, were successes. Cooper won an MTV Video Movie Award for Best Performance and a Screen Actors Guild (SAG) Award for Best Actor for his performance in *Silver Linings Playbook*.

Cooper carefully prepared himself for every role. He took dance lessons, studied with a Navy SEAL, and gained and lost weight. Cooper was starring in movies alongside famous actors, such as Robert DeNiro, Jennifer Lawrence, and Christian Bale. His dream had come true.

Cooper played Templeton "Face" Peck in
the action movie *The A-Team*.

A Famous Star

FOR MANY YEARS, Bradley Cooper was cast as the handsome male lead. Cooper wanted to experiment and to challenge himself by playing different roles. "Shame on anybody that's going to tell you who you are," he said.

Cooper challenged himself by playing a soldier
in the movie *American Sniper.*

In 2014, Cooper was cast in a role unlike any he had
before. He played Chris Kyle, a soldier, in the movie
American Sniper. The movie made more money than any
other film that year. Cooper won the MTV Video Music
Award for Best Male Performance. That same year he
became the voice of Rocket Racoon in the Marvel movies
Guardians of the Galaxy and Avengers: Infinity War.

Cooper co-wrote and sang the songs with
Lady Gaga for the movie *A Star is Born*.

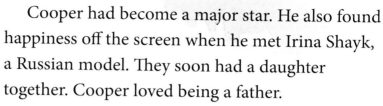

A Famous Star

Cooper had become a major star. He also found happiness off the screen when he met Irina Shayk, a Russian model. They soon had a daughter together. Cooper loved being a father.

Cooper had always been interested in movie directing. He decided to write, direct, and star in the movie *A Star is Born*. Cooper starred as a musician who discovered a young, talented singer, played by Lady Gaga. Cooper practiced with a vocal coach to change his voice. *A Star is Born* was a huge success. In 2018, it was nominated for three Academy Awards, seven British Academy of Film and Television Arts (BAFTA) Awards, and a Grammy Award. Cooper was the first person ever to receive so many nominations for one movie. The movie won the Academy Award for Best Film Music Award and a Grammy Award for Best Pop Performance.

Cooper was now one of Hollywood's highest paid actors. His movies have made $11 billion worldwide. Cooper wanted to use his fame and success to help others. Cooper started the One Family Foundation to help patients with cancer and donated money to charities that fight cancer.

Cooper snaps a picture with fans at the premiere of
A Star is Born in 2018.

Cooper uses the experiences from his life to help him act. He no longer just plays the good-looking boyfriend. "I've been a soldier, a musician, a chef, and a disfigured person," Cooper said. "I still want to play a conductor. And then . . . who knows?"

Today, Bradley Cooper is one of the world's most famous stars. As an actor and director, he brings characters and stories to life for audiences. He hopes to continue making movies for many more years. He loves showing people the magic of movies, just like he discovered long ago watching *The Elephant Man*.

Timeline

1975   Bradley Cooper is born on January 5.

1993   Cooper attends Georgetown University.

1997   Cooper applies to The New School.

1999   Cooper lands his first television role.

2001   Cooper makes his movie debut in *Wet Hot American Summer*.

2009   Cooper stars in the box office hit *The Hangover*.

2014   Cooper forms a production company named "Joint Effort."

2018   Cooper writes, produces, and stars in *A Star is Born*.

Career Highlights

Awards Won
- **1 BAFTA**
- **1 Screen Actors Guild Award**
- **1 Grammy Award**

Nominations
- **7 Academy Awards**
- **5 Golden Globe Awards**
- **1 Tony Award**

Total movie roles	**42**
Total television roles	**54**
Movie box office earnings	**$11 billion**

Find Out More

Books

Anastasio, Dina. *Where is Hollywood?* New York, New York: Penguin, 2019.

Garza, Sarah. *Action! Making Movies*. New York, New York: TIME for Kids, 2013.

Kane, Bo. *Acting Scenes & Monologues For Kids!* Burbank, California: Burbank Publishing, 2017.

On the Internet

Official Academy of Motion Picture Arts and Sciences Website. https://www.oscars.org

Official Marvel Website. https://www.marvel.com/characters/rocket

Works Consulted

Bradley Cooper. *IMDb*, accessed October 10, 2019. https://www.imdb.com/name/nm0177896/

The Official British Academy of Film and Television Arts Website, accessed October 1, 2019. http://www.bafta.org/film/awards/ee-british-academy-film-awards-nominees-winners-2019

Brodesser-Akner, Taffy. "Bradley Cooper is Not Really Into This Profile." *The New York Times*, September 27, 2018. https://www.nytimes.com/2018/09/27/movies/radley-cooper-a-star-is-born.html

Clapp, Susannah. "Bradley Cooper Reminds Us Some Stars Can Act." *The Guardian*, June 7, 2015. https://www.theguardian.com/stage/2015/jun/07/elephant-man-review-haymarket-london-bradley-cooper

Gross, Terry. "Bradley Cooper Learned to Sing, Direct, and Talk Deeply for 'A Star is Born.'" *NPR*, December 3, 2018. https://www.npr.org/2018/12/03/672848456/radley-cooper-learned-to-sing-direct-and-talk-deeply-for-a-star-is-born

Halls, Eleanor. "Bradley Cooper on Directing 'A Star is Born.'" *The Telegraph*, January 22, 2019. https://www.telegraph.co.uk/films/2019/01/19/bradley-cooper-directing-star-born-grueling-vocal-training/

Harkness, Jane. "Why Bradley Cooper Almost Quit Hollywood for Good." *Looper*, May 15, 2019. https://www.looper.com/142268/why-bradley-cooper-almost-quit-hollywood-for-good/

Martin, Rachel. "Bradley Cooper On the Personal Story Behind 'A Star is Born.'" *NPR*, September 14, 2018. https://www.npr.org/2018/09/14/647491779/bradley-cooper-on-the-personal-story-behind-a-star-is-born

Index

About the Author

Kerrily Sapet is the author of more than 30 children's books. She has written about presidents, queens, futuristic vehicles, athletes, and sneakers. Sapet enjoys watching everything from old black and white movies to superhero movies such as *Guardians of the Galaxy*. Her favorite movie theater snack is warm, buttery popcorn.